The Runaway Woods

The Runaway Woods

Stephen Sartarelli

Spuyten Duyvil
New York City

© 2000 Stephen Sartarelli

ISBN 1 - 881471 - 45 - 4
       1 - 881471 - 46 - 2 (hdc.)

Cover art by Sophie Hawkes, *Untitled*, monotype, XI-vii-1, 1994

Spuyten Duyvil
PO Box 1852
Cathedral Station
NYC 10025
http://spuytenduyvil.net

Acknowledgments

Some of the poems in this volume were previously published, often in earlier versions, in periodicals and anthologies to whose editors the author expresses his thanks: *The Literary Review, Alea, The New Criterion, American Letters & Commentary, Five Fingers Review, Talisman, Primary Trouble: An Anthology of Contemporary American Poetry*. Versions of some of these poems have also appeared in the chapbooks *Phantasmatikon* and *In These Skies*.

Library of Congress Cataloging-In-Publication Data

Sartarelli, Stephen, 1954-
    The runaway woods/ Stephen Sartarelli
        p.cm.
    I. Title.

PS3569.A734 R86 2000
811'.54--dc21   00-032989

Contents

NATURA MORTA

What eyes still glimpse the angels falling	11
Muted season evanescent	13
Pale wood browning	14
Light-riven, stalwart	15
Another dawn might be a spray of lavender	16
Another ravaged hillside gapes	17
Buildings rise nearly infinite in height	18
Shadows pock the furrowed slopes	19
In the rise and fall	20
Flat faces stretch to nether infinities	21
It was a kind of lilting madness	22
This sentence, like any, admits no delay	23
Silent craft with weightless cargo sail	24
Certain evanescences	25
Creaking lots, bird-scavenged	26
A hundred different shades of green	27
Seed flux and	28
A needle in the temple	29
Reason's graveyard in the window lies	30
Earthbound rings the heavens' thunder	31
Getting an edge on the tremors	32
A sudden turn toward another fog	33
The ragged matter at our fingertips	34
In the sudden throng of daylight	35

THAT LAND

1. Another way to anywhere	39
2. A sun of many minutes	40
3. Anything beyond	41
4. Whatever else the turning	42
5. Somewhere went the wending	43
6. Then a day removed, respite	44

7. *To this return*	45
8. *Another air recalled the water*	46
9. *The darker shade about the head*	47
10. *It must have been another country*	48
(coda) *Then away again, perhaps*	50

THE WELL

Hudson River Atony	52
The Well	54
Mistral	56
Residential Façade (Rome)	57
Confiteor	58
Saint-Estève	60

THE RUNAWAY WOODS

And now the hardened insistence	63
Phantasmatikon	65
Field	66
Wilderness	68
Winter Garden	69
In these skies invisible somewhere	70
Reading the Numbers	71
The Runaway Woods	72
The Medicine Wars	74
Arcana Mundi	76
Nostos	78

THE CIRCLES

Life Units	81
Acts of Light	84
The Silence Room	88
The Lost House	89
The Circles	90
Rochester	92
Middle Atlantic	93

Endymion   95
Acts of Light II   97

OPENWORK

(1) *Feathered wind, skylorn*   102
(2) *This effort then*   103
(3) *To a burning sky*   104
(4) *Elusive uplift*   105
(5) *By vapors white*   106
(6) *By changing water*   107
(7) *Iterant cloudbreak*   108
(8) *A momentary wind*   109

NATURA MORTA

What eyes still glimpse the angels falling
into blades of grass or flaming meadows
lie behind yet other masks, closed or squinting,
absorbing vision from the object seen:

the shattered mirror of the ocean's surface,
transmutation of the heavens in a momentary crease
of darkness in time's crossing with itself . . .

The crumbling walls along the old frontiers,
for all their preservation, recede with each new brick
laid carefully against the tide of years.

An uncast stone beside a ceaseless stream
gathers light like dust, witness or participant;
the sun that warms it is a mortal god, dauntless eye
of all the finite days of our bewilderment.

Muted season evanescent
in the clay's soft footing,
wordless call of day.

A gleam of dry rock
mosslike on the earth-bark
flashes from the latening,
no metal for the flint.

Cradle-bound and vertical
the green evades the gravity of water,
brushes lightly counterwind
anteceding fire
in a looming breath of sun.

Pale wood browning
in a void of labor
blind to crescent moons
concealed by daylight,
a hundred-year trunk
skin of no animal
plumbs the minutes
that ever remain.

A fallow stillness
time-wild, clockless
in a field eluding
torsion of the plow,
deliquesces airborne
ahead of any wind
of blackbirds
sombering afar.

(St.-Estève)

Light-riven, stalwart
in the profligate soil,
plane trees mar the inviolate sun,
the uncut branches burgeoning
in countless little germs of shadow.

Day teems protean inside and out
the boundary stones, tentacular
revision of the work of wind and hands.

Should an unexpected tremor of still other life
invert the bedrock under hills of pine
unwintered on a winter afternoon,
perhaps old seasons would reblossom nevergreen,
inward, earthward to some core of time,
some godhead buried in the wasted matter.

A momentary sky of azure spans the day untroubled,
though, as if to laugh an instant of eternity
upon the slow and imperceptible corruption
of a temporary birth, myriad and necessary.

Another dawn might be a spray of lavender,
soft grey in a labyrinth of branches
crossing black and bare in winter light,

a greenish lamp-glow bending shadow
and a hand still thick with sleep
toward absent suns behind the sky . . .

No sight returns the morning's gaze,
all renewing and renewed as if to mend
a broken circle binding earth and eye:

a late wind wafting darkness from the North
like smoke from burning capitals of light
cleaves the air with its brand of man-made heat,

stoking shades embedded in still sour shoots
oblivious to burdens of light to be shed.

(*natura morta*)

Another ravaged hillside gapes
in the crusted mask of ancient earth,
the old plow's furrow now but a scar
on skin shed centuries ago.

There is no stillness this twilight;
footpaths tremble under footsteps,
broom and wildflower cast their glow
with soft, indifferent violence.

Skies torn by half-seasons struggle
for the favor of the coming night;
loaded cars and trains speed to and from
the light, toward vanishing horizons.

A figure or two alone might throw
a benevolent shadow on the fields;
but en masse we darken everything,
except our own still shining heads.

(nocturne)

Buildings rise nearly infinite in height,
their interiors vast and grey like empty shafts
or cavernous warehouses where lovers seek
lovers lost down endless stairways darkening
in other, past dreams: a soul or two and I
ascend the void as though flying, propelling
the body up with each grip on the wall,
climbing with a force of wings or turbines,
aspiring to the end above, roof or sky
and then out, perhaps to the darkness of space

Shadows pock the furrowed slopes,
private forests draped in fog,
splendid houses hidden in the dusk.

The night glows with dog-eyes
ravenous for intruders,
tree trunks blacken the air.

The road clatters loud underfoot,
hard ground resists the hands
of daylight's golden promise.

Up the mountains hammers echo,
voices boom inside the quarries.

(americana)

In the rise and fall
of endless names
cited or invented
to round out a life
deemed perhaps too ordinary,
a single, soon-forgotten individual,
mother of a race of criminals, scion
of a neurasthenic line of forgers

might better color barkless trees
with a plurality of false descriptions,
forage for a hungry few or sate the masses,
than lie in bed and masticate
the synonyms for endless days and days,
orisons to little gods
of deprivation and despair

(predawn)

Flat faces stretch to nether infinities
below the city's wet surface.

Dark roots grope skyward,
a tree in bloom's a flailing hand,
age is innocence, youth corrupt,
days end with the rising sun.

Upside-down across the lateness
race the minions of another,
early life that crashes through
the shadows like a bludgeon.

A hint of pallor
steeling blue-grey in mud
only seems to usher in
another kind of night,

the blaring sleep, apneal traffic
of a fitful intermission
in the spectacle of daylight.

It was a kind of lilting madness,
a hammer to the taste,
that seemed to put an end to tapping
all the objects in the eye.

Some knew better, however:
a sour fume, acetylene perhaps
was found to have some value
beyond the usual dismay.

Where wider ways might lead—
down in lightness, many-sided
thirst—turned round and round
and now careers incessant,

though voluntary corners cut
may some day, even now
still offer an inverted chance
to reapply the turn more sharply,

restore the ravage to the touch.

This sentence, like any, admits no delay:
a little stirring here and there, perhaps,
to fool the neverending flow of blood,
but still the story races on and on . . .

A tiny point upon the arc, the flailing
stops at the moment of birth, as if unseen

Silent craft with weightless cargo sail
against the stony current, river of mud
winding grey and yellow in the dusk.

Time hastens late onto nowhere,
the day but one of countless separate worlds
along the darkening way.

At least the huge oaks still stand,
though they seem to fear the wind
as water fears heat.

A sheen of oil cloaks the ground,
makes walking precarious, slippery
from the rain of perpetual storms.

Certain evanescences
in broad rooms on the way to sleep
trip quick escapes like ceremonies
nonexistent neighborhoods
like someone else's memories

Such quiet couldn't be the cause—
just yesterday I quelled the eyelid
of a restless spirit sentencing the fluids
to another noisy, boxed-in afternoon

Perhaps the night itself gives passage,
safe-conduct between commas
then we halt as if commanded
on the brink of just the first ellipsis . . .

Sudden walls might soon collapse
if the next step were too sure,
too purposeful to dodge the necessary questions:
like pebbles tossed the mind rolls stair by stair
and down again to ground floors of pretended time—

There we shall not pass: front doors
open only darkness on our hoax,
chance becomes the only hope for consciousness;
another time the cold stone floor might pose
its period as termination of the thought—

but here the night air dashes everywhere, tepid, open-ended

Creaking lots, bird-scavenged
in early morning air,
provender of sunlight and the avid eyes
of multitudes in battle
for a momentary claim
to vision, space, tarnished prize
in the remaining corners of the memory—

Glass and black stone clash and merge
like natural phenomena,
cloudy vistas of another city
sliding off the surfaces
in blocks of living steel impressed on vegetation,
transparent citizens against the sky,
dogs on tree-trunks,
mortar on the faces of the passers-by.

How many green Arcadias
still flourish in the pockets of a hurried soul,
how many distant factories
come tumbling to the ground
behind the soon-forgotten thought
that shuts a waiting car-door
with a thud and plunges deep
into the as yet undiscovered treasures
of several billion pumping hearts
still waiting to be bled . . .

A hundred different shades of green
could never stay the builder's hand . . .

House in the grove, hotel on the mount,
salad-rich meadows frame eons of movement

and in the blur of achievement
all our loving plans grow thorns.

Pumpkinhead scarecrows speak to the land
a pity of creature to maker.

(diurne)

Seed flux and
Easter-light air
in time's loom

Black wind rending
time of unisense
time yet plasmatic

Ash-soil, not forever
but a lifebloody
soul-surface, lighting

every time, ever where
the earth can do
yet under heaven

All does regardless—

(der Liebestod)

A needle in the temple,
debris of ancient sleep pelting the mind,
eggs of presentiment hurled in fun
against the first to pass before
your sequestered eyes,
paperwork blasting in cahoots,
pyramid of hope
before the gawking millions,
one of the all-time greats.
How could they do this?
What kind of dream is this?
Der Liebestod, der Liebestod.
It's not a dream.
It's dreamlessness.

(nocturne)

Reason's graveyard in the window lies
tomorrowlike, curating a kind of thought
in the vapor of old toeholds, forever
to befriend refusal of the worst.

Continuance a barking roar of current
feeds a waking light like fish unknowing
in a net of sleep too large to see,

a wheeze of courtyard memories
in loops of frost and daftness tainted
even by time's passing in the dark . . .

Surely this is not the black and white of promise
in the sentences of misbegotten everyday—

Earthbound rings the heavens' thunder
blasted in a breach of azure yawning
in our well-familiar wall of thingness,
redounding silver in the emptiness . . .

To save itself a silly bird
might even doff the plumes of emperors—
and so we captivate the throng a moment
with all our fleeting matters:

the closer they come, the more like glass
they cast an image of encircling arms,
deaf and blind as all their vaunted knowledge,
naked in a hall of mirrors in the mind

Getting an edge on the tremors:
so hopes a lighter head
to gain in moments gaping
between steps to the floorboards—

oh the silly gods above—
could we expect any other
disruption in the day's recedings?

recognitions of another eye's
regard for love, touch or the main
required for a flight of years?

What finger-breadth of burning air
permits a flash of haloes in the mirror
can carry any old soul to term,
wing-effort against the wear and tear

A sudden turn toward another fog
or foreign signals trafficking in misperception,
warnings for the well-acquainted happen
almost out of season, at least in this
still kicking universe. Wherever
one may settle or lay pain to rest
with degrees of silence or noise on the run,
some larger, antlike purpose in the road
will take the convoys to their greener desert,
the tardy frost and unsuspecting flowers
fading only as the momentary music
of our gain. Some summer night a century ago
heroin was thought a panacea and the military life
a path to romance and supreme respect:
perhaps our cars will drive us all to heaven,
willy nilly, as long as every road
still seems to lead us where it's going.

The ragged matter at our fingertips
scoffs millennial at any measure,
unhewn form a fodder for the process
in a nutshell raised as monument,
microsecond brilliances falling as one
into the eddy of the present moment,
fatal pantomimes, dread as-ifs,
frantic figures dropping off, apocopate

In the sudden throng of daylight
rushing up to meet all comers
I doff the threadbare cloak of dreams,
walk through the press invisible
toward shadows in the backs of minds,
graves or pleasure-gardens teeming
breathless with another life

THAT LAND

1.

Another way to anywhere,
a runaway glance turning in,
the day without the benefit of time
or parting of earth for the fruit,
skies lost in the furrows:

to breathe the air is to pillage
the shadows, sentence the memory
to rigors on sensation's edge,
staccato of sunlight, draught
of sequels in the mirror—

wherever, in what secluded
passage named apart, thing,
unit, claim for staking, wrinkles
in a fold behind the letter,
dim socket of time's eye,

reap the tatters of direction

2.

A sun of many minutes
out of hand, animal oblivion
in particle and darkness,
again our rampant agonism
dies a good death . . .

The lurch of neverending days
careering blind to cities on the water
stopped, mature in silent abdication
of the burning green:
                        there the stone shies
down to earth from sky's caresses,

routs the genius of the place—

there the light dissolves whatever
does not slip the mind apparently,
shakes ideas out of effigy

3.

Anything beyond
the nothing when,
time-hum on a wing,
stillness troubled all
as one unique:

off the tender edge
tiding down, footloose
at a single point,
place of the fallow,
we rise away—

and there it went,
shuttling without,
around the earthen
mould of air, shade
of anything alone

where falling limbers up
the stasis of our birth

utters clouds upon a leaf

4.

Whatever else the turning
of a matter in a measure
out and over, seasonless along
the way beside the time without,

semblance, fugitive array of air
about a teeming vessel
lights upon the darkened hull
and there resides apart—

what other movement out again
to breathless space and privy
to the blood may carry light
beyond the gesture made and seen,

appearance less and more the time
still fret away the offspring
of the act:
        passing on alone
and back, sightless, it proceeds—

enfolded in its precipice
augmenting, now receding

5.

Somewhere went the wending
at the forking of the road,
terracotta as the ground
beneath the black of sense;

several steps ahead the moment
turned to something unexpected,
no longer empyrean blue

but colorless, ragged in time
beyond the frame, the blasted edge,
word-slave, centrifugal . . .

Elsewhere lay inconsummate,
time bedecked upon a hill,
away, amid chasms of ash
and walls of antic mortar

—In we go now, blithe
into the breach, head and hands
as motors on the hardened earth

6.

Then a day removed, respite
of fleeting penumbra,
in place anew, alone
yet one with the passing rest:

gestures in grass, frozen
in flowers, commemorative
hands on the table reach
for food of absent eyes:

wall of stucco humming white
in heat calm as the dead—
chipped plaster, wash of the waves:

forever high noon, silver dusk
a rasp of wind in air
but rolling like sand in ripples:

time and place
sheltered, sunbeaten in shadow,
attendant upon sight

7.

To this return
have steps as yet unmade
fallen into sudden place:

the crumbling vault continuous
in air and iridescence
houses only movement now;

all other refuge in the open field
demands a vegetal quiet—
there to thrive or wilt

beyond the garden's edge,
no light or shade to mark
the heated passing

8.

Another air recalled the water
wavering between the bluffs—

jagged as a glare effacing
distance on hot sand—

pirating the present in dream,
brutal as forgetting

where stone should say
what now eludes a waking eye,

what was it came away
and left the place as something else?

The light rages on in sleep,
time's old murderer,

progenitor, dove, blood-sister
come as on burning wings

9.

The darker shade about the head,
daybound, galing hard in empty
aspiration wakened only
in another moment's sleeping,
place on place inside and out
before the eyes, blasted, pristine
on a moment's sudden notice . . .

There would we flee:
                        above and past
the daybreak mountainsides recline
on treetops deepening in azure
for the chasing.
                    No mind for things
beyond our sliding fingertips—

a rumble of the body, mother-ship
of blight, rip-tide of years, quells
the squall, drowns the rattle of the open gate

10.

It must have been another country,
not the sea-cliff, not the evergreen
or cactus.
        Another breath of sense,
hours in a hand that cannot be,
I could never have said such a thing . . .

Innocence abjured under a sky
of trees, dome of eyelids,
areolae peering through cloth:
                        there
the fields of vision loom, centuries
about to pass to somewhere else—

rib of wood-grain, temporary
resting of the sap . . .
            And what then?
an airless visit to the marrow,
thunder from the missing thing?

Dark again, we swim back to shore . . .

It couldn't be the time again,
only sand before the glass:
never was the day so vast,
the land so light as ever
might delay our evanescence.

Pace, then, rise in shade away
from earthen grounding, course
on nameless bodies in the field—

whatever else may then arise
in breathing, in birthing fall away

coda

Then away again, perhaps
ahead to stone and water,
quicklime of another hand,
time's desire, little known—

just out of reach, the fading
forms as yet unmade about
a brood of light in shelter
see the day, born to none

THE WELL

HUDSON RIVER ATONY

Fort Tryon, Manhattan

There's a body in the river, unferried no doubt,
"believed to be a prostitute, name unknown,"
cursed or blessed (I've forgotten which part),
oblate in the winking sun of public images,
the shadow settling dustlike in tomorrow's sleep . . .

Across the shore, you can see the docks: bare masts
country-clubbing greenery against the cliffs—
oblivion the current or the wind
behind the roar of all our journalisms
jogging the memory or stuck in the craw,
the fragmentary views like dream-homes
raised in glass against the long bemasoned sky.

There at the bend, when the mist is thick,
you'd think the world had reached its end:
the gateway to infinity, sudden seesaw
over an abyss of green and concrete water,
checkerboard of pleasure-boats well on their way
to see George Washington amidst the ancient stone.

But perhaps infinity (or here at least)
is only the space between the certain charms
of old New Jersey's pretty face and what
we know to move within her entrails:
Rockefeller (which one?) bought that land,
say passers-by in admiration
of the distant bank they never reach.

And on this island maybe all the Madisons
and Lexingtons receding out of sight go on forever
only in some infinite regression, Chinese-boxlike
image of the image of the image of the thing itself
and so on to the sudden bend in vision
where only emptiness gives sign of something
other than the nothingness of not being the object.

Toward this frontier do we subject ourselves
to fight, feather-armed with ink of actuaries
turned against itself, shrikes of bloody stores
on bastions of invisible West Points
pushing paper toward the necessary fire of the eye,
fresh new versions of tomorrow and oblivion—

pencils shave, pages burn, staples grasp at air,
gloss fades to yellow after days of living-room sun,
a word or two begilded like the black stone in refraction
of an artificial twilight only seeming to give way
to another day or night, to continue all as if
it had always been this way before, cyclical,
or flowing like the river, dark and unimagined.

THE WELL

The words they spoke preceded them,
notions in the air or on the lips
of everyone to carry on the day,

a tipping hat or turning wheel
reflecting light or marking time
as naturally as the sun or moon.

And what a sun it was that shone,
an unexpected miracle
that in this season we should be so graced;

the energetic footsteps rained
as if to crack the hard, dry ground
reeling from that weight of promise;

a wind of everyday blew down
the chasm street and filled the banners
up to hang as on suspended sight;

debris on every side bedecking
champions of automotive ken
kicked up into the gust and swirled about

in whorls running off the train
like eddies off an ocean stream
and settled back into the flow

of profiles low and on the march
toward some still desired end
of movement seeming without end.

(I'm not the sort to criticize,
but to go on like this, like
fifteen thousand blind Bulgarians,

surely soon we'll meet our czar
with nothing for our eyes to see
but the road already traveled.)

And then that sun again, white
and seeming not at all to move,
like some glowing airborne milestone

for measuring the reach of possibility,
at least up to a certain point,
faint and as it were on the horizon,

where rising dust appears to form
a column in the sky above
a single spot in earth, a hole

the people circle round and round
as if around a waterwheel
to withdraw something from that pit,

water to sustain that endless turning,
to slake the endless numbers still to come.

MISTRAL

An occasional madness, airborne
from without the seeming calm
of light that softens even underbrush
and stones amid the evergreens,
peasant-house or crumbling fortress
fading ochre to white,
it arrives with a terrible hush
again, multimillenary, recurrent
moaning of the land in submission,
sightless rattle of secured shutters,
polishing the sky a glasslike blue,
thwarting life's heavenward reach to where
the trees still bend southeastward
even when the wind dies down.

RESIDENTIAL FACADE (Rome)

Dust on old festoons adorning the impassive stone
gathers unmolested by a slowly rising wind
that fades the burnt brown paint *intonaco*,
erodes the tiny lion-heads in single file in the sun.
Blind galleries repel the day, draw shadow
from the air that wraps their half-form in dimension
like a gift, sustains a solitary sparrow
looking to land, tentative, as it flutters past
a cold-eyed herm and up, to the hidden garden
sprawling green and unattended on the terrace-roof
beneath an open vault of blazing azure.

CONFITEOR

after Baudelaire

Seaside views are always overwhelming,
especially at certain times of day.
At dawn, when stretching east, the perspective
allows little more than blind surrender
and may even hurt, if the sky is clear
and gleaming hard and manifold upon the water.

And if behind the shore the land
soars sheer in crumbling bluffs where rocks
and jagged stones might fall at any moment
to the craggy beach like bullets from
the guardhouse of an angry *genius loci*,
then solitude will hardly seem a refuge:

the hum of the swell, the hush of the earth,
the stinging salt wind sweep away the dreams
of any soul for whom a little kicking
about the aging world is just a lesser form
of howling through the air in emulation
of the forces he would think to master.

Yet illusions readily relinquished
in the face of forces still much greater
do not die so easily, and joining with
the matter of their shaping and abuse
may further dwarf the dreamer, and rather make
his sleep the object of *their* monstrous thought:

What awe is this? Or is it pity?
The flaccid seastream belches up a tide
of swizzle-sticks and condoms, radios
and algae in a swirl of plastic bags
and tar, a wooden chairleg genuflected
beneath half a porcelain Venus . . .

Were the dreams that turned that leg the same
that blacken sea and sky? That wounded beauty,
sunlight bleeding between particles in air
that mirror and divide the attributes
of gods, itself can suck the very ghost:
the eyes soon tire, the mind flags in fits;

one might sooner twist that image further
or abandon it altogether
than try to fix it at a dying moment,
lest we too be sucked into the eddy—
make another question mark, Byzantine,
of the precious body, still vessel of all . . .

But perhaps this story can't be told at all;
perhaps the best thing is to run away
as quickly as possible, to seek out
the company of others and forget
how horribly complicated the sea
and dreams of mastery have become—

except I see their faces even now,
mooning between all the candy-wrappers
and seashells, casting long dark shadows
with each turn of the head, each cautious
gesture of friendship to the rocks and sand,
the absent billions, the empty sky above.

SAINT-ESTEVE

for A.D.

Another light defined the day,
the look of things, the way
a certain detail in the mind
or far away became the thing
it might have been for once:

a penchant in the jagged wind
of spores and other lives in air
and gravid in the colors of the noon
that change, sporadic, as they rise
or fade according to the time,

desires on a wing of green
above a bony land of rock
and rainless soil like the mortar
of immense constructions underground,
inverted monuments in earth:

no conjuration, simulacrum
of a budding oak or poplar
but a stone reflecting in the hand,
suspended in the tiny space
before the eyes, above the page

THE RUNAWAY WOODS

And now the hardened insistence,
the rock in the glass
that would swallow
every consummation missed,

the humid beguiling,
hands turned to tallow
to follow the chattel,
the done-upon smile, light
bled purple from the arm . . .

What were those clamorings,
the rabid guffaw,
acrobatics flying turn to turn
kaleidoscopic in heat?

Another slab laid on the couch,
windows open onto cloth,
hoop of the mouth slack
in dogged reconnaissance?

And then all the staggering rigors,
the fingers raised, driven
ragged right out of the jar,
spilled about on creation
for creation on hooks at the shambles—

What children might ever return
from that soil, what blasted
trees befit the middle line
cut deep in the germ?

The animals run round and back
and never round, never
turning but to end the turning,
race to the unfinishing

PHANTASMATIKON

for S.C.

From black against the nothing
hued upon the minutes
falling formless by the side,
beyond the choice of sight

the body and the field
momentary histrion
flexion of the ulna
rise toward the acid cast:

woman's breast or parry-thrust,
mirror-spawn, monster
of the act itself
the fight against the whiteness

freeze as if to be
an eye about to see below
the field of black and blank,
the body come *ex nihilo*

FIELD

The animals have fled
somewhere beyond the road.

A kind of haze, metallic
in occluded sunlight,
lies heavy on the eyes;

like an exhalation of the land
it softens the ground
to mud underfoot.

*

A group of people,
friends they say, lead me
past a field of stubble.

—There's the house, says one.
It stands dark along the path,
its windows deep in shadow.

I know all about
its sumptuous rooms.

It has no doors inside,
only open walls and stairs
that wander floor to floor.

They would take me there,
I know, but I have come
too far already.

*

Past the fallow field
behind the house
fences sink into the mud.

The land beyond swells up
into a dome of earth
where hidden rivers clash

and burst upon the plain
in gales of fire and water
from the passages below.

Where they might lead
I would follow in sleep.

WILDERNESS

As if there were no place
for errant eyes, visitors
to the moment unfolding.

What gods may dwell
or once held sway
here seem to flee
before all presence

or stir in sleep.

How could they sleep?
Surely the storms
the terrible seasons
assailing the temples

echo some breach
in matter's heart?

The people in the cities rage,
the people in the country rage,
bleed dry into fallow ground.

The land repels approach.

WINTER GARDEN

Hard upon unbreathing earth
a half-light turns the tilling hand
in darkness.
         Blasts of another sleep
scatter the shadows, unsheltering life
in flight from time in hot pursuit,
a sun gone black or red or white again—

and we act as if that eye can see,
break up rocks and force the seasons
round and round despite the rattle
in the night, as if to make a model
of fleeting resplendence, an impossible bed
of fireweed and forget-me-nots, planted
with the love of a gardner for the blind . . .

In these skies invisible somewhere
beyond the rooftops might be effigies,
jackals of the hour falling up
precipitous in air where sunlight
unshelters the blight from the blue,
the animal restrained in the genes,
on contact ethylene, bodies
swept up as the eyes withdraw
beneath the water in the blood . . .

their feet disperse at angles,
crisscross up and down as seasons,
phases of the moon or urgencies
of inconvenient homicide on wheels
amid the anaerobic signs of life:

this was the force irresistible,
this the magnet of the days awry,
the time so much of time
you'd think the air itself could die—

as clouds like white-clad nurses pass
across the unremitting yellow-green
of azure we would take them for flesh
but that they still seem to rise in glory
or die awash—
                 to these eyes,
double-winged against the wind,
black tunnel through the arcades,
chasm-windows on the soulless

READING THE NUMBERS

They have entered the house in broad daylight,
fifteen stories above a quaking sea,
raising the roof for no reason at all.
From the shadow-floored hell of the hallway
a sudden start is the only escape,
a hand on the stair or return to the dark,
but even then the dirty work goes on:
the elevator is out of order,
the children sit out in the car all day,
the finch I held in my hand on the way
bursts into flame with each flutter of wings.
From the bar we hear the men rummaging,
glimpse a lawn of sea-green waves, flashes
on the water swelling up to the house.
In the mirror above your head I see
tongues of fire raging in the background,
though silently. It is too late. The land
provides no refuge, no images seen
from the road and cherished as they vanish.
Our only haven may be the garage,
far from the rafters, the terrible sun,
safe from the mayhem above and below.

THE RUNAWAY WOODS

Perhaps the old morning imbalance
still quickens the gut
to draw tired saplings
back into light, slough off
yet another soul abandoned
like Moses to rage stone by stone,
life by indifferent life.

Perhaps the frantic images,
the broken lines about the face,
besought to cage the tender
palpitations so weak in the hand,
will yet dam up the coursing universe—

from that distant world the forms swell
fat and menacing, the voices rasp
indistinguishable in deceit,
the ragdoll masks fall flat
while the flailing begins
in the proximate void
as if to steal time with a yowl
and bend space back into fiefs.

And yet sometimes the daylight creeps so gently
through the filters of existence
that it seems one could go on forever repeating
the life-spanning gestures of heat and regret—

as if the endless recitation
of words that mean "bread"
were each time raised anew
against the hunger, the murder, the wear and tear
blazing a trail through the runaway woods . . .

As twilight teeters between empty chairs
we would burn before the hiding guests
returned to have their day in anguish.

Peace, it seems, we'll entrust to heaven
and leave the bartered calm to cushion
yet another evening.

THE MEDICINE WARS

The numbers turned out to hold nothing
but a vague indication to the body,
index extended, wrist beganglioned
in timely service to the treadmill
of bright futures always round the bend

and at that arrow's point the thing
exploded, searing shut the walls between
one eye and the next, world-compartments
that would suck the soul inside to nothing,
mouth a fleshwound open to another vacuum.

The real support came buttresslike
from props and sticks, gnarled and forked
at various points under and beside
the carcass, there to lift unto another
day the life within, the life within
the life, the roar inside the ears . . .

And there the wires pulled and pulled
and then relented, and then pulled again,
and sometimes sounds emerged, sometimes
clicks or music, and the counting never stopped,
the numbers rolled across the rippling contours
of the hour and bottled the remains
and called it time, space, thought—

Never on those distant seas
shalt thou set sail again,
nor shall thy cursèd spawn
set foot upon the land beyond . . .

Flesh so gently turned upon the bone,
furrows in the bedrock like the shade-extruding
orifices cut into the face of day
gape with the night of their passages
away, eroded dark into the minutes . . .

Enamel, too, gives way with time
and once again the vision glooms
or loses its bite: at one corner
as a leg begins to totter, the bend
would bring the whole damn picture down
with it, smoke and mountains, pullulating
pockets deep inside the voice remaining,
were the succor not impeccably well-timed.

But that was taken care of too.
Quadrant by quadrant, and the prospects,
by all accounts, look good.
There will always be some virgin land untrod,
however infinitesimal. You can always divide
and subdivide. The counting never stops.

ARCANA MUNDI

    At times the inefficient organism
can bear the weight of ages—

        the sinew plied, recast
to move a soul in space.

    Lives flee unmemoried as words
with each breath out from under,
  vanish in the air unbidden—

    winged worms, futurity
the noisy god, consume again
  the ashes consumed.

    The unfinished work,
beyond the glass.
        The severed breast,
the cloven brain.

    There are no secrets left
to shine upon our nakedness:

the frost under the open sky
    burns the lips
before they would speak:

    May we sleep forever
    as the gravid burgeons
    of our population,

shudder in the dark,
to keep the eyes sealed

beyond the kicking feet.

NOSTOS

Revisiting the sites of our abandoning,
we pass through spirit-holes we left behind
in all the objects now bereft of charm,

trains of ghosts like cherubim in caracol descent
upon the falling step raise heavens
on the pavements of our passing, bridging fast
the gaps receding from one subdivided moment
to the next diminishing of life.

Aura, you might call it, or redolence
beyond the fragile walls that hold the force
that brings the moments momentarily together,
love or longing as the principle
unfolding all that space a millionfold
or more, eternally should time permit . . .

And after, do the minutes scatter yet again?

And will all the places once blest
fold up again upon themselves to nothing?

THE CIRCLES

LIFE UNITS

Unwrought, the old stone
blazes under currents
of star, counterfort
to time, handwork
through the spheres

*

Whatever were source
before the making,
luck spinning non-atoms
shadow where nothing
wasn't but became—

we would call
the absence light

*

Matter rechanged, reflections
in a god's eye recast material:

time solid, built to the number,
flux immured:
               thus do I murder
the door, spiral wreckage
of a father's head unsexed
golden, resplendent—

and thus the flowering,
myriad, unique
ad infinitum

flaming obstacular
earthwise through ether

       *

Porous vessel, translucent
bridge—bodily pass
the phases, humorous
by daylight's mooning, leaden
or rank by heat's corridor:

all would flood the open dark,
kiss the moment's sleep
unmoored forever—

time fed in the drift, befallen

*

And then night, quags
of particle unrest
seal water's womb

people the terror
in passing life,
earth unanimal,
shade recumbent

*

From sleep rain
the minutes undoing,
amplex of half-light
and shadow falling
dayward into sudden
eclipse—
        air and light cast
blood and breath (the final
inversion), earthen rush
into time's wedge, mass
disprisoned.
        The fire
within the seed, lymph
or poison, burns
forward and back

ACTS OF LIGHT

1.

With shadow sky
filaments the dark
behind the day's weave—

ground-break reflection,
rime of the gloom,
round of earth brooding
for ages at once—

hard in the sediment
another manifold
resplendence of passings

where thundering pendant
in stone recedes
time-dark, hovering
in descent—

Then airbound
returning, movement
as wind from stone, as sap
shadows lightward,

space bodied forth,
emplaced.
         Extending
untimely, selfwise,
transpiring

2.

Of single form
bereft, bright in the hour
of its passing

till the many
fall away
as one again

flat on a wall
of past
indeterminate

earth enfolding
its own elapse,
the telling in retelling,
breathing to eclipse
regenerate

darkening in birth

3.

From matter chance
forever green among the stones
unravels shadow, canopies
for light escaping
offspring of another day,
where ever were never
                        but for then,
timely refrain, *envoi*
to another youth—

godward in obliteration
of site, reenacted
till stone were turned again
in air, finally
unhoured

4.

And if the turning out
of this unfolding
were nothing but
(the telling)—

earthbound vapor cast out
of the houses of its flesh

as if to drive light
ever inward, past reflection

penetrate the hand
to further moment,

condensation of the thing,
time-harvest?

THE SILENCE ROOM

for S.

A blur of trees
window-streaked by houses
leaning fast away
and gone before the eye
can rest,
   escaping
in a glint and hum of bodies
lurching row by row
in flight, it seems, from safety
or what one might call home.

Here you travel light
or naked, with nothing to carry
but yearning or fear.

A thousand trains race hard
in your direction,
through the cars you hurtle
to the back, against the onrush,
to silence:
   a room, perfect
and square, lone woman sitting
calm in empty space.

Such light and relief,
and nobody else.

The silence washes over the eyes
in ripples, like sleep.

Perhaps this way lies home.

THE LOST HOUSE

Seemed the trespassers
might rape the penates
before any mother-spirit
came to call the place home

Seemed another order
—flash and jolt,
rack and minister—
held the lever, just
to flip the blue sky
subterranean—

The life, the love,
the infinities hulled—
the pith in the pot,
salvation on wheels,
move on to the next—

but to let our hands
burn in the open,
looking back from the plain

           and still
to hold out for
some small rooftop corner,
sun-ravished like the reeds
that drink below,
meet for the hungry,
a glory of kings

THE CIRCLES

In some great clatter unremarked
the wheels abrade across our mother land,
the quiet night a whirlwind of small demons
on the road about what tree might still
have soared ahead of an imagined time . . .

Awful children of the hour—

gently we lift them against the sun,
toss them high into the air . . .

How easy to avoid their burden,
how deep their shadows overhead.

To other lights we would consign
the journey of our fingertips, through cracks
within the sky above, sun-maddened, multiplied,
to regions of the skull where crowns
of music spill apart to no conclusions,
silent fire on the rooftops, open arms
across the churning fields, pray for us . . .

Our spinning worlds
unknowing fast
ungenerate outside the shelters
clapped together one-two-three;
only as they fall away
do we begin to see
what in our momentary madness
had escaped us—

Time and again
the windows fill with dying suns
before they can be opened, apples
fly onto the branches of another age,
children leave the houses of their nightmares
for headspinning lawns of oblivion;

time and again return the animal
restrictions, mouth to the wind,
teeth champing on a bloody light
in blurring seasons, back and forth
across the tide of numbered floods

and in those breaking circles like the day
reborn ass-backwards in the West
the stars still lose and find us
yet again along the way to Thule
or Finisterre, trip the grinding wheel
of night against the splitting air,

no comfort for speculation
or distracted minds at home—

Perhaps one day they'll guide the skylong
roots of wayward plants

and we shall suck the tainted flowers

ROCHESTER

What in that old gorge,
outflow of an underland
breach, yellows now
with not so ancient violation,
reeling ghosts of red moon
and silence disanimate
insidious in a wheel
no longer turning in the light
of day, tall revival carapace
shot with sky-blue,
once industrial?

MIDDLE ATLANTIC

My cold hand
I could extend
to the glistening surface,
touch the invisible curve,
hold again
        what wrinkles
on the water would
like trembling cataclysms
wring a moment
from the air.
        Tempered roar,
frail vibrato.
        Here lies nothing
but what turns again to nothing,
oblivion rebirthing
reobliterated.
        Fire blue
as ocean, wave upon wave
on hinterlands reflected
in the shadow-swell.

Havens burning.

Wind-crevice, solar abyss.

Oil of endeavor watered
down, perhaps, to reconception
of those galaxies perpetually falling

insubstantial gas or fluid
off the tables of the hour,

dragged forever through
this life.
        That passage
of my waiting.
              What birds
fly above the foragers?

What green fades colorless
against the light?

What rain shall rise again,
what ocean fall
and hurl itself upon the sky?

ENDYMION

Too many moons
I'd counted on
to cleave the night air
in the absence
of another light
to sleep by.

Now days careen
and crash into the dark
without the benefit
of eyes to guide them
to a proper end.

The aimless paths
of hours passing
open doors that
weren't there before
and cease to be
when opened.

Time reverts to
emanations of the
moment unobserved,
illuminating ways
unfollowed,
decisions left
to the impending sun,

silence turning
anywhere beyond
the seeming nothing,
shedding darkness
out of sight until

all were light, blue
light, unchanging as
my open eyes,
yet to be seen.

ACTS OF LIGHT II

1. *riverside*

On claylike water
now half-giving
shadow as blue-grey,
reflection shrouds the distance,
diffuses light in deference
to particles in air,
steel of aircraft
nearly vanishing
above the weighted convoys
moving on the painted ground.
Round in circles or
straight on ahead or out
to sea or inland go
the flashes of a sun
half-hidden in the haze,
no telling what old fire
stoked in that dark agitation
might not sear
the very water's skin.
Wings of heat uplifting
seagull and pigeon alike
as hawks above
a preyless waste,
blind inertia driving
the great human masses
to new destinations atomized
within the void
of their geographies:
jagged cities out of reach,

oceans scented in the river-sludge,
moons dispersing in the glare—
ripples in the surface
of a stream that seem
as if unmoving or just
moving in a single place,
each alone with its reiterating
pattern of darkness and light,
its fleeting imitation of eternity.

2. *seaside*

No ears for all the thunder-shells
no shadow anywhere

no rattle of still burning wheels
beyond the edge of sky—

no flesh on elevations of the deep,
architectures we've bereft—

No figure on the waves
no tritons at her water-feet—

a gasp unlistened-to,
no fishes in the rain—

no one in the open air,
a circle of the iris falling,

no breath behind the mist,
electric there, we have gone now,

there, may we now rest
in shadow without shadow

no blanket on the earthen hull,
no fireflies on open lips,

a ghost of coral centuries
adrift, forever wanting

3. *offshore thundercloud*

Glistening seclusion
bright extent
vault without key
unbuttressed, drumless
vapors aloft
and eyes on the ground
cathedral of air
credo of light
I believe what I see

OPENWORK

(1)

Feathered wind, skylorn
on eroded arches
sun-riven, echo
of elapsing light
on edifices ringing
light for light recovered
in the air above
the curving clay

(2)

This effort then
to silence in
reverberation
of the hammer
startles stubborn
matter suddenly
apart in frictive
bursts, the drop
that follows down
eluding repercussion
of the act
to beckon sound
away with it
becoming but
for once
a vacuum
like the void
before creation

(3) (Venice)

To a burning sky
unfolding in cascades
of bells and wingless bodies
ghosted light, pressing
fast the opening
less matter than the air
itself, the hands now drop
their burden to unsteady
ground and strain to join
abruptly soft, inobdurate,
by thundering remotenesses—

All those instant eyes
in a turn of the shoulder—

What awful winds abroad
about the shrunken universe

(4)

Elusive uplift,
dark return, overstep
out of the drift,
another recess
of the open
on elements unmooring
a rise of water and flesh—
tremulous eyelight
diaphanous
incarnate

(5)

By vapors white
concealing white
and evening the outline
offered in extension
of embracing light
by blood and heat,
the vision planes
about unbreaching
what perspective obscures
to the intending eye,
debris of apparitions
wrung from atoms
only soft as exhalations,
muscles bent as starfall
under clouds

(6)

By changing water
drift in passages
receding hours
on forgotten mud,
earth-dome at rest
on a heavenlong breath,
day's empty square
to fill without
the things envisioned
body, stone, relief
shadow the recess
from firelight vapor
vegetal aflame
with air, moonrise
for bedeviled dust

Brick by brick
the minutes abdicate
the soil's memory

Void by void
the constellations steal
into the stars

(7)

Iterant cloudbreak,
glancing voices
absences between
lines vanishing
tectonic or botanical,
earth-deep, daylong
in retreating order
by invisible command,
past or hidden
in time or light
whispering continuance
to clay and teeming cell
by the damp onset
of morning to be
burned away
as other ages
in stone

(8) *for J.H.*

A momentary wind
accorded life or art

the forms enabled
by the gesture's shadow

outline the grace
that would dispel
the dust or green ethereal—

a scattering of bodies
undeterminedly reeling
out into the air
of their corruption—

What agonies of respiration
in a moment's grip,

spectrums of the never seen
turning in a bending
of the sun

NOTES TO THE POEMS

page 15. Saint-Estève is a large, ancient estate in Provence, home to an English painter and friend of the author.

page 55. The "fifteen thousand blind Bulgarians" were soldiers who suffered a crushing defeat at Belasitsa in 1014 at the hands of the forces of Byzantine emperor Basil II (known as Bulgaroctonus, the "Bulgar-slayer"), who put out the eyes of the fifteen thousand prisoners taken in that battle, leaving one one-eyed man for every hundred to lead them back to their tsar Samuel. The Tsar fainted at the sight and died of grief two days later.

page 56. The mistral is a cold, dry northerly wind that blows down the Rhône valley into Provence. It is reputed to drive certain people temporarily mad.

page 57. *Intonaco* is the finishing coat of fine plaster applied both in fresco painting and on the facades of many Italian buildings. The paint applied fresh to it bonds with the plaster and tends to change in color and texture with time and erosion.

Stephen Sartarelli was born in Youngstown, Ohio, spent much of his youth between the U.S. and Europe, and has been living in or around New York for the last twenty-two years. He is the author of *Grievances and Other Poems, Phantasmatikon* and *In These Skies,* and the translator of many Italian and French authors past and present, including Gesualdo Bufalino, Francesca Duranti, Umberto Saba, Casanova, Xavier de Maistre, Jacques Cazotte and Pierre Klossowski. His poems and articles have appeared in a variety of periodicals and anthologies.